Inside My Body

How Do My Muscles Get Strong?

Steve Parker

www.heinemannraintree.com
Visit our website to find out
more information about
Heinemann-Raintree books.

To order:
☎ Phone 888-454-2279
💻 Visit www.heinemannraintree.com
  to browse our catalog and order online.

© 2011 Raintree
an imprint of Capstone Global Library, LLC
Chicago, Illinois

Edited by Kate de Villiers and Laura Knowles
Designed by Steve Mead
Illustrations by KJA-Artists.com
Picture research by Mica Brancic

Originated by Capstone Global Library Ltd
Printed in the United States of America by Worzalla
Publishing

15 14 13 12 11 10
10 9 8 7 6 5 4 3 2 1

Library of Congress Cataloging-in-Publication Data
Parker, Steve, 1952–
  How do my muscles get strong? : muscles and exercise /
Steve Parker.
      p. cm. — (Inside my body)
  Includes bibliographical references and index.
  ISBN 978-1-4109-4017-9 (hc) — ISBN 978-1-4109-
4028-5 (pb) 1. Muscles—Juvenile literature. 2. Exercise—
Juvenile literature. I. Title.
  QP321.P277 2011
  612.7'4—dc22   2010024800

Acknowledgments
The author and publisher are grateful to the following
for permission to reproduce copyright material: Corbis
p. **17** (© Randy Faris); Getty Images p. **25** (AFP/Patrik
Stollarz); NASA p. **13**; Photolibrary pp. **4** (Corbis), **8**
(Phototake Science/Eric Grave), **11** (Photoalto/Odilon
Dimier), **12** (imagebroker.net/Uwe Umstätter), **15** (Somos
Images), **16** (Moodboard RF), **19** (AFLO Royalty Free/Koji
Aoki), **18** (Polka Dot Images/Jupiterimages Jupiterimages),
20 (Imagestate RM/Adrian Peacock), **23** (Medicimage),
27 (Image Source).

Photographic design details reproduced with permission
of Science Photo Library p. **6** (Gustoimages); Shutterstock
pp. **15**, **18**, **25** (© Isaac Marzioli), **15**, **18**, **25** (© Yurok).

Cover photograph of boys flexing muscles reproduced
with permission of Getty Images/Workbook Stock/
Jupiterimages.

We would like to thank David Wright for his invaluable
help in the preparation of this book.

Contents

Words that appear in the text in bold, **like this**, are explained in the glossary on page 30.

How Strong Can I Get?

Most people can become very strong! Strength depends on muscles. Everyone has the same number of muscles. Everyone can make their muscles bigger and stronger by using them regularly, keeping active, and getting exercise.

Pull harder! A tug of war is a tiring test of your muscles' pulling power.

What do muscles do?

Muscles make you move. Without them, you could not walk, eat, write, or even blink. Every action you make is muscle-powered. Without the muscles in your chest, you could not breathe. Even your heart, which pumps blood around your body, is a muscle.

deltoid

pecoralis major

deltoid

triceps brachii

biceps bracchi

rectus femoris

gluteus maximus

biceps femoris

This is what your muscles look like under your skin. Some of the main muscles have been labeled with their scientific names.

How Many Muscles Do I Have?

The human body has more muscles than most people think—over 640! Some are big and powerful, especially those in your back and legs. Others are tiny and delicate.

Movement muscles

Your body has about 300 muscles that attach to the skeleton. These are called **skeletal muscles**. Each muscle is joined to a bone at each end. As the muscle pulls, it moves the bones and that part of your body. Skeletal muscles are also known as voluntary muscles, because you can control how they move.

A CT scan "sees" inside the body. In this view, the large blue areas are muscles in the hips and upper thighs. The two big, greenish-yellow parts are the thigh bones.

Other kinds of muscles

Your body also has about 300 more muscles inside organs. These are called **smooth muscles**. There is also one very special muscle, which the heart is made from. This is called **cardiac muscle**. These muscles are involuntary muscles, which means they work without you thinking about it.

Muscle names

Every muscle has its own scientific name. Often this describes its size and shape, and perhaps where it is in the body. Some muscles also have everyday names. The table below shows some of these muscles, and what their names mean.

Everyday name	Scientific name	Where are they?	Meaning
Pecs	Pectoralis major	Upper chest near each shoulder	*Pectoralis* means "to do with the shoulder." *Major* means "big (muscle)."
Delts	Deltoid	One over each shoulder	"Shaped like a triangle"
Glutes	Gluteus maximus	One in each buttock	*Gluteus* means "to do with the buttocks." *Maximus* means "biggest (muscle of its type)."

What Is Inside a Muscle?

Muscles come in many different sizes and shapes, but inside they all look very similar. The main parts inside are bundles of **muscle fibers**, which are thinner than hairs.

SCIENCE BEHIND THE MYTH

MYTH: If you don't use your muscles, they disappear.

SCIENCE: If muscles are not used much, they become smaller and weaker. But they never disappear. If you start to use them again, they soon get bigger and stronger.

🔍 Look at **skeletal muscle** under a microscope and you see a striped or banding pattern. That is why this type of muscle is also known as striped or striated muscle.

Fibers and fibrils

Bigger muscles have more fibers than smaller muscles. As you exercise your muscles, they get bigger by growing more fibers.

Inside muscle fibers are bundles of even smaller string-like parts called **myofibrils**. These fibrils contain long **protein filaments**. It is these protein filaments that can make a muscle **contract** (get shorter) by sliding past each other. Inside a muscle there are also **blood vessels**. These bring high-energy substances for the muscle to use as it works.

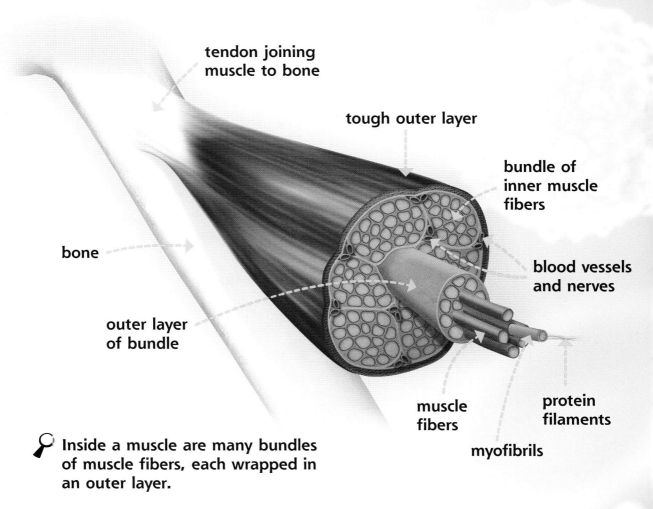

tendon joining
muscle to bone

tough outer layer

bundle of
inner muscle
fibers

bone

blood vessels
and nerves

outer layer
of bundle

muscle
fibers

protein
filaments

myofibrils

Inside a muscle are many bundles of muscle fibers, each wrapped in an outer layer.

How Do Muscles Work?

Muscles work in a very simple way. They **contract** (get shorter). As **skeletal muscles** contract, they pull on the bones. Strong, rope-like parts called **tendons** join muscles to their bones.

Pull not push

Try bending your elbow. The biceps brachii muscle in your upper arm contracts and pulls your lower arm bone. You can see and feel the biceps bulge as it contracts. But the biceps cannot push to straighten your elbow, because muscles can only pull. So another muscle on the underside of your upper arm, the triceps brachii, pulls to straighten your elbow.

tendon

triceps brachii contracts

elbow joint

biceps brachii relaxes and is stretched

tendon

triceps brachii relaxes and is stretched

elbow joint

biceps brachii contracts

This diagram shows how your arm muscles contract to bend or straighten your elbow.

Teamwork

All over your body, one muscle pulls a body part one way, and then another muscle pulls it back. In fact, for most movements there are not just two muscles but 10, 20, or more. They work as a team for smooth, steady movements.

Working out with weights makes the shoulder deltoid muscles and the biceps brachii muscles bulge.

11

How Do I Keep My Muscles Healthy?

To stay healthy, muscles must be active. They need to make movements and get exercise. Lazy muscles become weaker and less healthy.

🔍 **Cycling and skateboarding with friends is a great way to be active.**

Action all day

Sports and exercise are very good for muscles. Apart from organized sports and exercise, there are many ways to keep your muscles active in daily life. For example:

- Cycle somewhere (if it's safe) rather than go in the car.
- Use the stairs instead of an elevator.
- Keep on the move while out with friends, rather than sitting around.
- Help with chores at home, rather than sitting in front of the computer or television.

Many benefits of exercise

Sports and exercise help your **skeletal muscles**, and they also have many healthy effects on the rest of your body.

- Your heart stays strong and beats powerfully.
- Your breathing muscles work well, so your lungs take in enough air.
- Your joints stay flexible and bend easily.
- Busy muscles use energy from your food. If this energy were not used, the body would store it as fat.

SCIENCE BEHIND THE MYTH

MYTH: Astronauts take it easy in space.

SCIENCE: Not true! Astronauts have lots of scientific work to do. They also get plenty of exercise, using equipment such as exercise bikes. This is because there is no pulling force of gravity for their muscles to work against. Without exercise, their muscles would soon become weak.

What Is Good Exercise?

Almost any kind of exercise or activity is good for your muscles and your body. But certain kinds of exercise and sports are better than others because they involve many muscles around the body.

Regular and often

- Exercising regularly or playing sports three or four times a week is much better than a long session once every few weeks.
- To have the best effect, exercise should last at least 20 to 30 minutes.
- The activity should be hard enough to make you breathe faster and speed up your **pulse rate**. This shows that the exercise helps your heart, lungs, and your whole body.

SCIENCE BEHIND THE MYTH

MYTH: Exercise is a waste of energy.

SCIENCE: Wrong! It's natural for the body to use lots of energy by moving around and staying active. Exercise is not a waste of time or energy. It keeps the body healthy.

Special exercise

Some people need to exercise only certain muscles—for example, if they have an injury or disability. A cycling machine makes the legs work well while protecting a back injury. Swimming helps to keep muscles busy while supporting a painful joint.

Practical advice

Warm up, cool down

Athletes do gentle warm-up exercises such as bending, stretching, and jogging before they start training or playing. These exercises gradually get harder. This helps prepare the body for the main action. Afterward, cool-down exercises prevent muscles and joints from becoming stiff.

Which Sports Are Best?

Most sports are good for the muscles and the body. But not all sports suit everyone. Each person should try several sports or games, to find the best one to keep fit and have fun. If you find a sport or exercise too difficult, you are probably less likely to continue with it.

🔍 **Swimming is a good all-around form of exercise that involves most muscles in the body.**

Everyone is different

Organized sports are a great way to exercise muscles and stay healthy. Because everyone is different in body size, shape, and abilities, certain people are suited to particular sports. For example, a short person might not be good at basketball, but could be good at long-distance running. A person who is not so skilled at ball sports might be a great swimmer. It is a matter of finding the best sport for you.

Having fun

Sports and games are also helpful because they can be satisfying and fun. People try to do better each time they play. In team sports, you can make friends and enjoy helping the whole team win.

 We are the champions! It feels great to take part in a sport.

 SCIENCE BEHIND THE MYTH

MYTH: It's best to have lots of bulging muscles.

SCIENCE: Not always. It depends on the sport or exercise. Long-distance runners do not usually have lots of bulging muscles. In fact, many of them are very slim and light.

What Are Muscle Skills?

It takes more than just strong muscles to be good at sports and exercise. Muscle skills are also important.

Practice

Most activities and sports need good reactions, timing, balance, and coordination to help muscles work together to make movements smooth and accurate. For example, to catch a ball, you move your hands to the correct place, watch the ball go into your hands, and grasp the ball at the right time. This is known as hand–eye coordination.

Practical advice

Practicing muscle skills

Throw a tennis ball against a wall from about 3 meters (10 feet) away. Try to hit the same spot on the wall every time and catch the ball as it comes back. After 20 throws, take a step back and repeat the exercise. As you keep practicing, your hand–eye coordination will improve.

Coaching and equipment

People do better at sports and games if they learn them the right way. This usually means having a trainer or coach to give advice, show you the correct way to do things, and help you avoid problems such as strained muscles.

The correct clothing and equipment are also essential—not only for better performance, but also for safety. For example, in organized cycle racing, everyone has to wear a helmet. The right kind of equipment, along with coaching, practice, and avoiding risks, all make sports much safer.

A skier's amazing balance develops over years of practice.

Do Muscles Get "Hungry"?

Your muscles need fuel to power their movements. The fuel comes from the food you eat. This food energy is brought to muscles through the blood. It is pumped by another muscle, the heart, which also needs a fuel supply.

🔎 **This sprinter's muscles are working hard to help him run fast.**

Blood sugar

The main food substance that muscles use for energy is **glucose**. It comes from the breakdown of substances called **carbohydrates** in food. When in the blood, glucose is usually called blood sugar or blood glucose.

Muscles need another substance to break apart blood sugar and get energy—oxygen. It comes from the air you breathe into your lungs. The oxygen goes from the lungs into the blood, which takes it to your muscles.

Aerobic exercise

As muscles work harder, they need more blood sugar and more oxygen. So the lungs and heart work faster in order to supply the extra blood carrying oxygen and glucose. This type of activity, using lots of oxygen that the body gets by breathing harder and faster, is called **aerobic** exercise.

SCIENCE BEHIND THE MYTH

MYTH: Snacks are bad for you.

SCIENCE: Not always! Fruit and some sports bars usually have energy that the body can use quickly. Other foods, such as meat, do not provide energy quickly. Very sugary snacks such as chocolate are not very good, since the body cannot cope with lots of sugar in a very short time.

Which Is the Most Important Muscle?

One muscle in your body never stops working. Your whole body depends on it. This muscle is your heart.

A bag of muscle

The heart is like a bag of muscle. It pumps or beats at least once every second. During each beat, the heart first fills with blood. Then it **contracts** powerfully to squeeze the blood out along the **blood vessels** to all body parts.

Extreme body fact

The heart's beating speed can be measured by the **pulse rate** in the wrist. This varies depending on people's age, fitness, whether they are female or male, and what they are doing.

- Young babies have a rate of 110–120 beats per minute.
- This slows to about 60–80 for an adult at rest.
- Jogging puts the pulse rate up to 90–100.
- Very hard exercise increases pulse rate to more than 150.

Faster and harder

Like other muscles, the heart needs plenty of regular activity to stay strong and healthy. This is why sports and exercise are good for the body.

SCIENCE BEHIND THE MYTH

MYTH: Eating too much before exercise is bad.

SCIENCE: This is true. After a big meal, lots of blood flows to the stomach and intestines, to collect the digested food. This leaves less blood for the muscles and brain.

The way the heart beats during exercise can be watched on a screen to make sure all is well.

Which Problems Affect Muscles?

Muscles can suffer injuries and other problems, just as other body parts can. But usually muscles heal well, with no lasting effects.

Pulls, strains, and tears

A pulled or strained muscle happens when the muscle tries to work too hard and some of its tiny **muscle fibers** are damaged. It may also happen if the muscle is stretched suddenly, such as in a fall or accident. It usually mends in a few days. A torn muscle is when many tiny fibers break. This is more serious than a pull or strain. A bad muscle tear may need an operation to join the torn parts with stitches or clips.

SCIENCE BEHIND THE MYTH

MYTH: People shiver when they are scared.

SCIENCE: Some people think we shiver when we are afraid. But usually it is when we are cold. Shivering is what happens when muscles twitch. As they twitch, they give off heat that warms the body.

Painful cramps

A muscle cramp is when a muscle tries to **contract** on its own, without you wanting it to. The muscle becomes hard and painful. A cramp may happen when you suddenly use a muscle a great deal, after not using it much. The muscle quickly becomes very tired. Another reason is when the body loses lots of water—for example, as sweat—and the water is not replaced by drinking. This is known as dehydration.

Practical advice

How to ease a cramp

If you have a cramp, try to stretch the body part so the muscle is pulled longer—a friend can help to do this. Rub or massage the muscle.

How Do I Take Care of My Muscles?

Busy muscles are healthy muscles. If you keep on the move, stay active, and get regular exercise, your muscles will be fit and strong.

Making faces

Apart from the big muscles in your legs and arms, there are hundreds of smaller muscles all over the body. More than 50 are in your face, including muscles in your lips, cheeks, eyelids, and forehead. They need to keep active, too. You use them to eat, drink, wink, blink, talk, raise your eyebrows, smile, and frown. To see them at work, look in a mirror and make some funny faces!

Extreme body fact

The smallest muscle
The body's smallest muscle, called the stapedius, is not much bigger than this letter "l." It's deep inside your ear. Its job is to pull on the tiny ear bones when sounds are too loud. This prevents too much **vibration** of the ear bones, which might otherwise cause ear damage or even deafness.

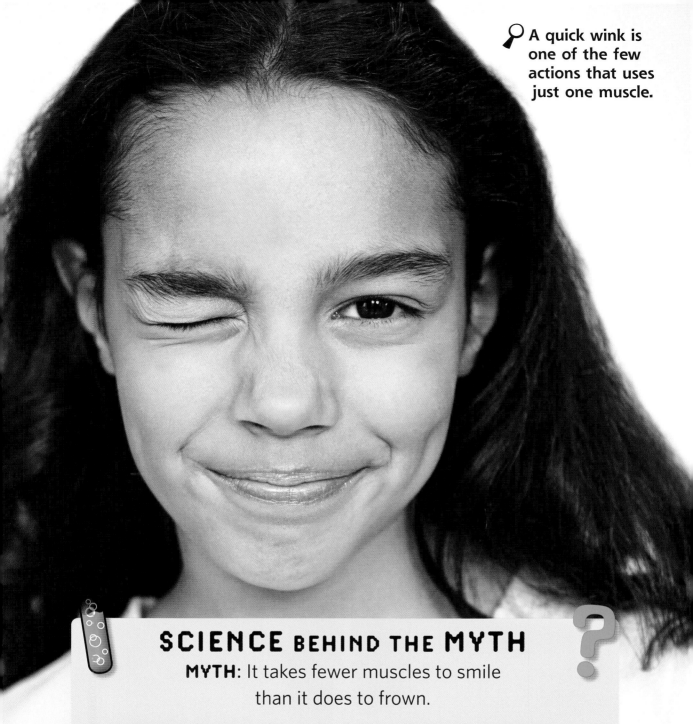

A quick wink is one of the few actions that uses just one muscle.

SCIENCE BEHIND THE MYTH

MYTH: It takes fewer muscles to smile than it does to frown.

SCIENCE: Scientists disagree about whether people use more muscles to smile or to frown, and it takes different amounts of effort to make a small smile, a broad grin, or a big frown. However, if you smile and are happy, you are more likely to be active, rather than sitting around doing little with your other muscles.

Your Amazing Muscles

The muscle that can bend the most is your tongue. Some people can curl their tongue into a U shape or an upside-down U!

The eyelid muscles blink around 10,000 times each day.

The muscles in the forearm that bend the fingers are called digital flexors.

Your longest muscles are the left and right sartorius. Each one stretches from your hip down your thigh to your knee.

Your strongest muscles for their size are the temporalis and masseter, on each side of your head. They work your jaws so that you can eat.

To nod and shake your head, you use muscles in your neck.

The forearm muscles that straighten the fingers are called digital extensors.

You sit on your biggest muscles. They are the two gluteus maximus muscles, left and right, which are in your bottom.

You stand on tip-toe by **contracting** your calf muscles.

Glossary

aerobic process that needs oxygen, such as aerobic exercise

blood vessel tube through which blood travels around the body

carbohydrates in food, substances containing carbon, hydrogen, and oxygen, which includes sugars and also starches in foods such as rice, potatoes, and pasta

cardiac muscle special kind of muscle that makes up the walls of the heart, and which never gets tired or fatigued

contract to get smaller or become shorter

filaments long, thin strands, such as the protein filaments inside myofibrils

glucose sugar, the main energy-providing fuel for muscles

muscle fiber thin, string-like part that forms bundles inside muscles

myofibril extremely thin, long strand that forms bundles inside muscle fibers

protein substance that forms many parts and structures inside the body, including skin and muscles

pulse rate number of pulsations or bulges per minute in the body's blood vessels, usually felt in the wrist, that shows the heart's beating rate

skeletal muscle muscle that pulls on the bones of the skeleton; also known as striated or voluntary muscle

smooth muscle muscle with no pattern of striations or bands seen under a microscope; also known as involuntary muscle

tendon strong, rope-like part that joins a muscle to a bone

vibration when something shakes very fast, usually many times

Find Out More

Books

Burstein, John. *Mighty Muscular-Skeletal System: How Do My Bones and Muscles Work?* New York: Crabtree, 2009.

Parker, Steve. *Move Your Body: Bones and Muscles* (*Body Talk*). Chicago: Raintree, 2006.

Spilsbury, Louise. *The Skeleton and Muscles* (*The Human Machine*). Chicago: Heinemann Library, 2008.

Websites

www.bam.gov/sub_physicalactivity/
Visit this website to get ideas for the best ways to exercise and stay healthy.

http://kidshealth.org/kid/stay_healthy/fit/work_it_out. html
Check out this website to find out why exercise is cool!

http://yucky.discovery.com/flash/body/pg000123.html
Get the lowdown on muscles at this website.

Index